The Dog Who Saved the Bees

Written by Stephanie Gibeault
Illustrated by David Hohn

Published by Sleeping Bear Press™

The sun shimmered.
The bees buzzed.
Hundreds of hives needed help.
Cybil Preston got to work.

As chief apiary inspector for the Maryland Department of Agriculture,
Cybil guaranteed the health of all the beehives in the state. And right now,
she needed to inspect hundreds of hives before they made a cross-country journey.

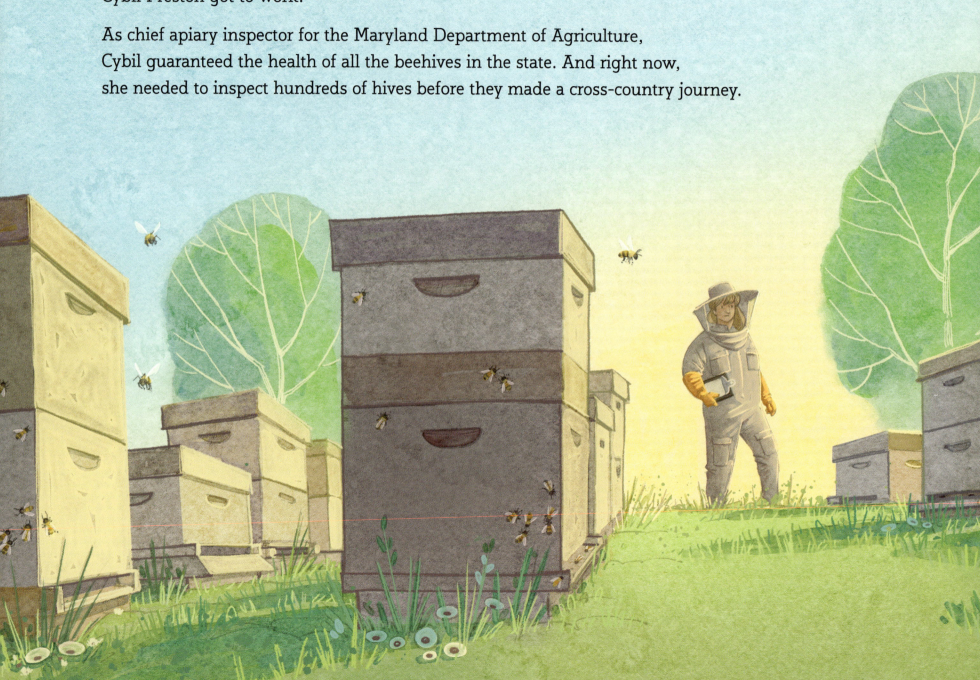

Farmers from the East Coast to the West desperately needed the honey bees to pollinate their crops. Otherwise, there wouldn't be enough foods like apples, almonds, and strawberries for people to eat.

The bees were in danger of contracting foulbrood, a deadly disease with no cure. It was so contagious that if even one infected hive left the state, it could wipe out entire bee populations.

Cybil had to open each hive and inspect every frame inside, and there were more fields to go. Winter was only a few months away, and opening the hives in the cold would harm the bees.

Baby bees that die from foulbrood stink like rotting roadkill. Dogs have amazing noses that can detect even the tiniest trace of foulbrood in a closed hive. Could a *sniffer* dog be the answer to saving the bees?

Cybil already had three dogs, but they were all too old. She needed to find a young dog that could be trained for scent detection.

Then, at a beekeeper Christmas party, she heard about Mack.

Because he was rowdy and wild, Mack's owners kept him in the garage. Nobody to play with. Nothing to do.

When Mack met Cybil, it was love at first sniff.

Thump. Thump. Thump.

Mack's tail wagged so hard, his whole body shook.

Cybil couldn't bear to put Mack back in the garage. Although he had no manners and no training, her heart broke for the lonely dog. She had to give Mack a chance.

Nobody came to say goodbye.

At Cybil's house, Mack had space to run free.
There were rules, but Mack ignored them.

"Sit," said Cybil.

Mack wandered away and sniffed the grass.

So many new sights and smells.

He wanted to explore, not pay attention. If Mack couldn't focus, he couldn't inspect beehives. But Cybil couldn't adopt *another* dog. Mack was her only hope.

Cybil refused to give up. Maybe there was a way to teach this distracted dog to concentrate.

Mack loved to play fetch. So Cybil threw his ball.

Again and again.

Day after day.

Then, before she threw, she said, "Sit."

Mack learned he had to sit before he could chase his ball. Slowly but surely, he focused more and wandered less.

Now it was time to start scent training with a trainer.

Mack greeted the trainer, but then a leaf blew across the field.

OH NO! Mack chased after it.

The trainer thought Mack was too easily distracted.

"Your work is cut out for you," he said.

But Cybil refused to give up. She needed Mack's help and so did the bees.

Like before, Cybil turned scent detection into a game.

She hid a foulbrood-scented rag inside Mack's favorite toy, and they played fetch with it. Soon Mack learned to love that stink so much that he drooled whenever he smelled it.

Finally
Cybil and Mack
were ready to work with the trainer.
But the rules of the game had changed. Now, instead of being stuffed inside his toy, the scented rag was hidden somewhere in a large warehouse.

"Find it, Mack." Cybil pointed down an aisle.

Sniff. Sniff. Sniff.

Mack searched up, down, and back again. There were so many smells—musty, metallic, and stale. But Mack refused to give up.

Wait.... There it was!

Mack sat in front of the hidden rag to tell Cybil what he'd found.

"Good boy," said Cybil. She threw his ball to reward him.

Now could Mack find the smell of foulbrood outdoors in an *empty* beehive? There were so many distractions.

"Find it, Mack," said Cybil.

Mack paused. He had never searched these boxes before, but he knew those magic words.

Sniff. Sniff. Sniff.

First box—nothing. He stopped.

Cybil pointed to the next box. "Find it, Mack."

Sniff. Sniff. Sniff.

There it was! Mack sat.

Mack and Cybil trained hard for nine months. Mack learned to listen. He learned to focus. And he learned to locate even the tiniest trace of foulbrood. But he still wasn't finished. Now he had to prove it. He had to pass a scent-detection test.

On a rainy fall day, the examiner hid nine foulbrood-scented rags in different cars in a junkyard.

Cybil's heart raced. There were so many new sights and smells. Could Mack focus enough to find every rag?

"Find it, Mack," said Cybil.

Mack wandered between cars. He sniffed unfamiliar smells. He shivered in the cold. But he refused to give up.

Sniff. Sniff. Sniff.

Mack searched bumpers, doors, and tires. There it was—faint but clear. He sat next to the hidden rag. One rag down, eight to go.

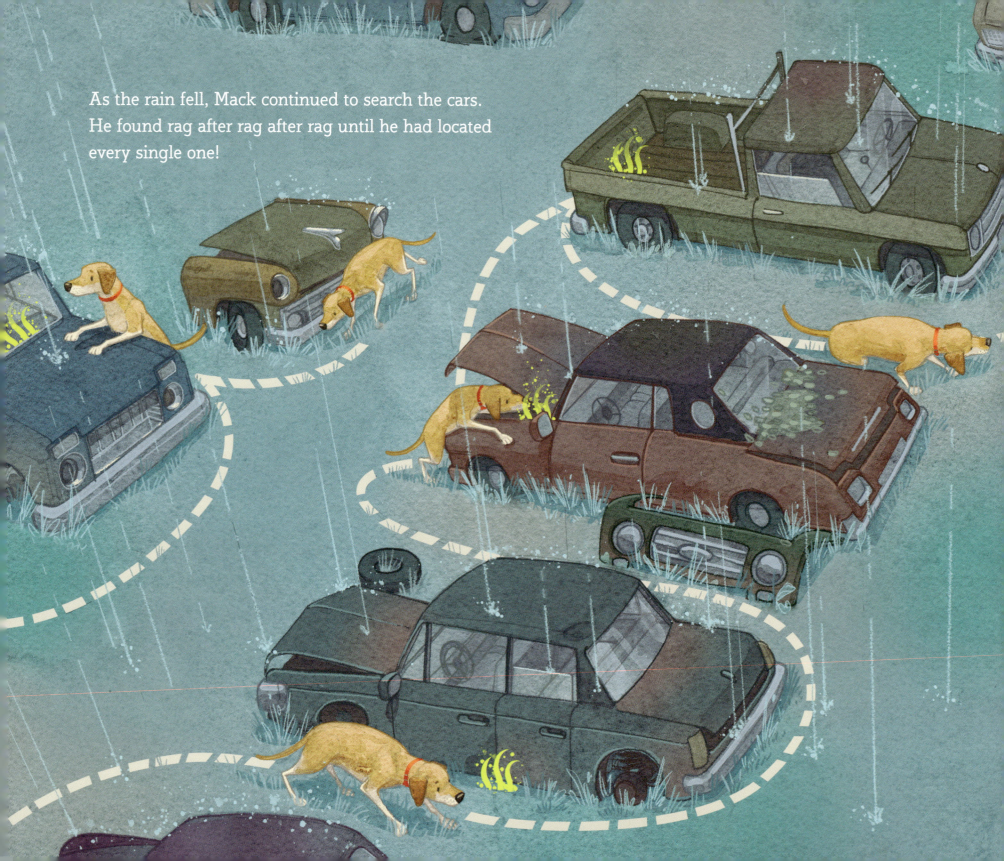

As the rain fell, Mack continued to search the cars. He found rag after rag after rag until he had located every single one!

Mack was certified as a scent-detection dog—the only one for foulbrood in the *entire* country. He lapped up whipped cream from the coffee shop to celebrate.

The real test came a few days later when Mack went to work with Cybil. For the first time, he faced a hive full of bees.

Mack stared at the wooden box in front of him.

Buzz. Buzz. Buzz.

It made a strange noise.

"Find it, Mack."

Aha! A new sound, but the same game.
Mack lowered his nose and went to work.

A bee sat in the grass.

Cybil ran to comfort Mack. If he became afraid of bees, he'd stop inspecting hives. They'd come too far to fail now.

Cybil tried again at a quieter hive. "Find it, Mack."

Mack hesitated, his tail low. But Mack refused to give up.

Sniff. Sniff. Sniff.

Mack searched the hive. Then another. And another. He inspected every hive in the field. All of them were free of foulbrood.

Cybil beamed.

Mack spent the cold winter sniffing rows and rows of hives. His nose searched more than 1,600 hives in a single month! Thanks to Mack, the foulbrood-free bees were certified safe to travel across the country to pollinate food crops.

That May, Mack and Cybil received the Customer Service Heroes Award from the governor of Maryland.

"Look, Mack. You're a hero. You saved the bees!"

Mack wagged his tail. Cybil had found her detection dog, but Mack had found his home.

The winter sun shone.
The bees snoozed.
Hundreds of hives had help.

Mack got to work.

Dogs serve people in many jobs. There are guide dogs for the blind, explosives-detection dogs, and search and rescue dogs. Bees also serve people by pollinating our food supply. I think training a dog to help bees so bees can continue to help humans is a perfect fit.

I met Cybil Preston in 2018 when I interviewed her for a news article. I was fascinated by her job and touched by Mack's rescue. As a dog trainer, I wanted to know more, so this book was born.

The Maryland Department of Agriculture used beehive-sniffing dogs from the 1980s to 2014 when the last one retired. That's when Cybil took over as chief apiary inspector. Thanks to help from K-9 trainers like Major Mark Flynn at the Maryland Department of Public Safety and Correctional Services, Cybil was able to get the former program up and running once again. After working for nine winters, Mack retired in June of 2024. Now Cybil and her second bee dog, Tukka, are working together to make a difference for honey bees.

You can help bees too by planting window boxes or gardens full of native bee-friendly plants. Grow those plants organically, without the use of chemicals that can harm insects. And you can celebrate World Bee Day every May 20 by telling your friends, family, and even your government about the value of bees and the importance of conserving them.

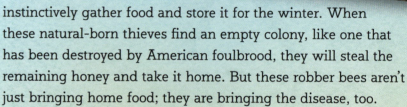
Mack inspecting a hive wearing his official apiary inspector bandana.

American Foulbrood and Bee Survival

American foulbrood (*Paenibacillus larvae*) is a highly contagious bacterial infection that kills the larvae (baby bees) of honey bees (*Apis mellifera*). Once a colony (the group of bees that lives inside a beehive) has been infected, traces of the bacterium, known as spores, can be found in not only the beeswax and the wooden hive box but in the honey as well. These spores stick around for up to sixty years.

Cybil training Mack on an empty beehive.

This is a deadly problem because honey bees instinctively gather food and store it for the winter. When these natural-born thieves find an empty colony, like one that has been destroyed by American foulbrood, they will steal the remaining honey and take it home. But these robber bees aren't just bringing home food; they are bringing the disease, too.

Although a new vaccine for honey bees helps increase their immunity to American foulbrood, there is currently no cure. To protect healthy bee colonies from an infected hive, beekeepers must destroy the diseased colony and burn the frame and other wooden hive parts. That means when Mack prevented the disease from spreading, he saved beekeepers money and time. More important, he saved bees.

Why Does Mack's Job Matter?

Worldwide, farmers rely on bees to pollinate more than 130 different crops, including nuts, seeds, fruits, and vegetables. Without bees, many delicious, healthy foods like blueberries, cucumbers, and watermelons would never make it to your table. But it's not just local bee populations doing the pollinating. Honey bee colonies are portable, so commercial beekeepers ship their bees all over the country to farmers with crops in need of the bees' services. Flatbed trucks carry honey bee hives along highways from state to state. One truck can carry millions of bees. It's essential that these bee colonies don't take any hitchhiking diseases with them on their travels.

That's where Cybil and her bee dogs come in. A bee colony doesn't leave Maryland unless Cybil and her human and canine inspectors have determined it's healthy and free of American foulbrood. But human inspectors can only open the hives and examine the colonies when the temperature is above 60 degrees F (15.5 degrees C). That's when the bees are active and flying about.

Mack and Tukka don't have bee suits like the humans, so the risk of stings is too high for the dogs to work in the summer. However, colder weather is perfect because the bees stay clustered together for warmth *inside* the hive. Cybil uses the bee dogs' noses to inspect closed hives when the temperature drops below 52 degrees F (11 degrees C). Opening the hives for human inspection during this time would be harmful to the bees. Thanks to the bee dogs, Cybil can conduct inspections year-round.

American foulbrood is rare, found in less than 0.05 percent of inspections, but bee dogs are essential in finding it. Mack could inspect fifty colonies in ten minutes with perfect accuracy. That would take Cybil an entire day. So the next time you sit down at your kitchen table, say thank you to the bees and thank you to Mack and Tukka for all their hard work.

How Does Mack's Nose Know?

Although Cybil can smell rotting larvae infected with American foulbrood when she holds a chunk of honeycomb, she can't smell tiny traces inside a hive. She uses her eyes to look for infected larvae. So how does Mack do it? Well, dogs have an ultrasensitive sense of smell.

A dog's nose is designed for scent detection. Slits at the side of each nostril allow a dog to exhale air without disturbing the scents in the air that were just inhaled. And that inhaled air is split into two streams—one for breathing and one for smelling.

Mack and Tukka waiting to inspect a field of beehives.

Plus, compared to your nose, the inside of a dog's nose is lined with millions and millions more scent receptors, special cells dedicated to noticing odors.

All those special features wouldn't be useful without a brain to interpret their findings. Both humans and dogs have an area of the brain devoted to understanding smells, but the proportion of that area is much larger in dogs. With a design like that, it's no wonder Mack's nose knows.

Selected Bibliography

Aizen, Marcelo A., et al. "How Much Does Agriculture Depend on Pollinators? Lessons from Long-Term Trends in Crop Production." *Annals of Botany*, vol. 103, no. 9, 2009, 1579-88, DOI: 10.1093/aob/mcp076.

Craven, Brent A., et al. "The Fluid Dynamics of Canine Olfaction: Unique Nasal Airflow Patterns as an Explanation of Macrosmia." *Journal of the Royal Society Interface*, vol. 7, no. 47, 2010, 933-43, DOI: 10.1098/rsif.2009.0490.

Dickel, Franziska, et al. "The Oral Vaccination with *Paenibacillus Larvae* Bacterin Can Decrease Susceptibility to American Foulbrood Infection in Honey Bees—A Safety and Efficacy Study." *Frontiers in Veterinary Science*, vol. 9, 2022, DOI: 10.3389/fvets.2022.946237.

Horowitz, Alexandra. *Being a Dog: Following the Dog Into a World of Smell*. New York, Simon & Schuster, 2016.

Morse, Roger A. and Calderone, Nicholas W. "The Value of Honey Bees as Pollinators of U.S. Crops in 2000." *Bee Culture*, vol. 128, 2000, 1-15.

Rosell, Frank. *Secrets of the Snout: The Dog's Incredible Nose*. The University of Chicago Press, 2018.

Wilson-Rich, Noah et al., *The Bee: A Natural History*. Princeton University Press, 2014.

ACKNOWLEDGMENTS

Thank you to the Maryland Department of Agriculture and Cybil Preston for allowing me to share this story. Cybil generously gave me hours of her time for interviews and discussions about Mack and his training. To make a donation to the bee dog program, please contact the Maryland State Beekeepers Association about their Apiary Inspection Fund.

Mack's retirement party.

To Cybil and Mack
for sharing their story and saving the bees
—STEPHANIE

To my mom.
"If you don't bother that bee, it won't bother you"
is still sage advice.
—DAVID

Text Copyright © 2025 Stephanie Gibeault
Illustration Copyright © 2025 David Hohn
Design Copyright © 2025 Sleeping Bear Press

Publisher expressly prohibits the use of this work in connection with the development of any software program, including, without limitation, training a machine learning or generative artificial intelligence (AI) system.

All rights reserved.
No part of this book may be reproduced in any manner without the express written consent of the publisher, except in the case of brief excerpts in critical reviews and articles. All inquiries should be addressed to:

SLEEPING BEAR PRESS™

2395 South Huron Parkway, Suite 200, Ann Arbor, MI 48104
www.sleepingbearpress.com © Sleeping Bear Press

Printed and bound in the United States
10 9 8 7 6 5 4 3 2 1

Library of Congress Control Number: 2025005310
ISBN: 978-1-53411-332-9